Travis C. Patterson

CoachTCP's

PlayBook
To Getting An Interview

I0494688

24 Hours

Or Less

How To Get An Interview In 24 HOURS OR LESS

The Instant Interview Success System

(1)

By Travis C. Patterson

How To Get An Interview In **24** HOURS OR LESS

The Instant Interview Success System

CoachTCP

The Career Professional:
Travis C. Patterson

Cover Design: Travis C. Patterson
Interior Design: Travis C. Patterson
Photo Author: (1) Front Cover Clock In Hand ©2008-2023, Brandon Dahlberg
2020 Edition: Travis C. Patterson Editor
[2] Photo of Man In Waterfall by Jose Murillo, Unsplash

[3] Graphic Design By Travis C. Patterson

[4] Photography By Travis C. Patterson

[5] Spreadsheet, Travis C. Patterson

[7] Exert from the Inauguration of John F. Kennedy's Speech

[9] Picture: Karate Nurse, Kill Switch (The X-Files) A virtual Dana Scully attacks a nurse in Fox Mulder's AI-controlled reverie. The scene is made by a freelance animator and received praise from several critics.

Wilson Resume Writers is now known as PRR Training & Consulting.

Forward:

You will have interviews requested in 24 hours or less because this system is proven to work by thousands of people just like you and me. I have acquired success on both sides of the interview desk as an applicant and interviewer. Email me to enjoy a full year of interview coaching to help you be more successful in the interview process.

*You are never alone in this process. Always use your resources at your immediate reach and acquire any through research and plane ol' asking around. Think of me as your Human Resource, your **Interview Coach**, and we will find this journey more exciting than how you started it.*

If you have issues in your past that are holding you back, remember, it is not always about how you start, but ALWAYS IN HOW YOU FINISH. Start finishing today, with me, CoachTCP. My team and I will see you at the finish line.

Travis C. Patterson
info@TheInterviewAccelerator.com
Free Trial:
www.theinterviewaccelerator.com/7-day-trial-the-interview-accelerator/

How To Get An Interview In 24 HOURS OR LESS

The Instant Interview Success System

To My Mentors

I thank you for all you have taught me in coaching. The knowledge and understanding you have imparted to me is a great help and support throughout my career. I believe my success is at least in part due to your sincere support and mentorship.

I express my deepest gratitude for believing in me. You each are excellent friends, teachers, mentors, and great inspirations for me. You inspire me to pursue my goals with hard work and dedication. You show me the value of honesty, sincerity, and trust in coaching, business, and building productive relationships.

I appreciate and value everything you taught me. Those lessons will forever remain significant contributions to my success and achievements. I aspire to forward your kindness and wisdom to every life impact today. I choose to be the difference that we would like to see in the world.

Thank you once again for your time, support, and patience.

Ethically,
Travis C. Patterson

(1) *(3)*

Take This Playbook With You On The Go!

If you loved it, please let me know. Tune in to our Podcast and Youtube to learn about negotiating your salary and more.

(1) (3)

PREPARE

Quote's On Identity

"Knowing yourself is the beginning of all wisdom." - Aristotle

"At the center of your being, you have the answer; you know who you are and you know what you want." - Lao Tzu

"When I discover who I am, I'll be free." - Ralph Ellison

There are three things extremely hard: steel, a diamond, and to know one's self." - Benjamin Franklin

"Once you identify who are, only then can you determine who you are not" - Tawanda Auston, Small Business Owner

"What kind of man do you want to be? With that answer, I will show you the kind of man your son will look up to." - Bettie Patterson, Mom

These quotes are from people that have made an impact on the world that I know. Most of us take more time getting to know other people more than we know our self's. We can watch television, YouTube, and Facebook to learn about what the famous are doing in the gym or their businesses.

We watch the sports and memorize statistics on the greats who play the game. To bring this example closer to home, some of us pay more attention to our coworkers than what we are doing.

Being jealous, envying, or even paying the compliment of being a copy-cat is not going to bring us closer to our career goals. We should take a moment to get to know ourselves before spending another 3 hours or year on someone else's life.

Most of us interview more times in a lifetime than actually accepting real jobs. There can be anywhere from 3-10 other job interviews before starting the one that wants you to start working for them for every job. So, why not try to improve this process, shorten the search, and improve the search results with more intentional responses.

Who are you? Who were you when you made the most money? If this is your first job, what kind of path will I start? A businessman once told me that the job immediately after college is the most massive stepping stone because it will determine your career growth direction.

The truth is that we work so many jobs before we get into our careers because we don't know who we are yet. We tend to work on the things that we are good at until we discover what we are great at.

When we discover what we are great at, that magical moment is the first day of our career. For some of us, that next step could be to go to school to further your path to growth in your field. Let's talk about degrees.

A degree qualifies you for an entry-level position in various industries. Do not be disappointed if you don't get the

Executive Level $90K opportunity you wanted first out of school.

Ultimately, discover who you are, what you are great at, and your value in your industry. When you find out how valuable and defined you are, you begin to think that maybe you need to go where you are more valuable to be whom you need to make the money you desire to make. So, who am I?

I am someone that has been fired from more jobs than I ever left on good terms. I am someone that has tried different careers like I was on a buffet line.

I am someone who has interviewed for more jobs than actually getting promotions from them. **WHY WOULD I TELL YOU THAT!?!?!**

I had to be honest with myself for me to find what I was great at. One of my coworkers from a retail job I once had yesteryears ago asked me every time they saw me, "Where are you at now?" My friend suggested these two things, (1) that I couldn't keep a job, and (2) the **BEST AT GETTING JOBS.**

The one thing that I was GREAT at was my Achilles Heel. **My greatest strength was also my weakness.** I think I didn't last long on my jobs because I wasn't satisfied with the pay. Other reasons could have been leadership, training, growth opportunity, responsibility, and of course because I knew that If I didn't like the job that I was on, I could just get ANOTHER ONE.

These statements are my truths about my past. I was also at a point where I honestly didn't know myself either. I found that I cared more about my client's well-being rather than their purchases. I always needed to go beyond the purchase for client satisfaction and over-deliver on value.

I listened to people and didn't want to repair problems, but rather fix them so they would tell their friends about me and not see me again for a long time. *I found that customer service was my GREATNESS, my Gift, and my Genius.*

Once I discovered that I went from making $5.25 an hour to $50 an hour, to $145 an hour. I found that I was wasting my time if I wasn't making someone else's life better. So who am I?

I am someone that discovered that I was pretty knowledgeable and well-practiced in the entire employment process. On top of that discovery, I recognized that I cared about people.

Through my growth in customer/client services, I found my way in HUMAN RESOURCES. I will never forget the conversation that confirmed my beliefs. "Travis, we need to talk after your shift," my employer said.

Ohhh, I was nervous because I was sure of what I thought was going to happen next. I just knew that I would need to go home and start looking for jobs again. "Travis, thank you for your work here at the company, but… Here is a raise in your salary and a contract for your new permanent position! Here is the address; sign this paperwork, and we'll see you tomorrow On-Site!" she said to me.

So yeah, that is a little about how I have spent successful time on both sides of the hiring desk. So, who are you?

What to expect through the process of this book?

First of all, thank you so much for purchasing my first book. **You** will find my best techniques and the foundation of how I started interview coaching. Your goal is to get an interview.

What will you expect? You will refresh your fundamentals and learn who you are as a professional. The secret of getting an interview in only 24 hours or less will be revealed shortly through these simple steps, preparation, planning, practicing, and performing.

How you prepare for an interview, for a career, or job will determine the actual health of the journey of your career.

If you have already started, remember that preparation doesn't always occur in the beginning. Project management has taught me to re-evaluate your steps at several points to reassure you finish where you need to be. It's important about how you finish.

The truth is, many people never plan their steps out professionally. You reading this book is why you will be more successful than the other people applying for the dream job you want.

So what will you need? You would need this book and the courage to step out of your comfort zone. You will find charts, graphs, and strategic career counseling that will land you in the best position possible. Before we get too deep, I would like to clarify that attitude is everything.

How you perceive, intake, and digest information in your life with ALL of your mistakes will be everything. In this book, you will find mistakes that I have made. You will also find all of my best techniques that scored me positive relationships and instant results that established healthy paths to my career.

(4)

So what is an interview, and what is its purpose?

An interview is a meeting between two or more parties with goals and intentions for each other and the person interviewing.

There are usually two parties involved during the interview process, the interviewer and the interviewee. The interviewer wants to know are you the right person for the job, the company, and if you can do the job?

(4)·

As the interviewee, you ultimately want to know do you want this job. Can I do this job? Does this job offer me the opportunities to reach my goals professionally and personally?

Some simple things to do to prepare for your interview is to read the job description and to learn about the company.

If you have an opportunity to establish connections and relationships with key people in the company or department, ask them about the job and the interviewer.

Define your circle of connections and resources. Find out who are the ***who's who*** of your network. Someone in your family or friends or social media or even associates may have a way to get your foot in the door with a job you want.

Practice interviewing. You may feel silly in the mirror, but you should want to introduce yourself to yourself a few times and try to record yourself and see how you look and how you sound. If you don't want you, why should the employer?

Be confident but not too confident where you oversell yourself. What will you wear? How will you smell? Do you have enough gas for your car? Will it rain that day? Do you have an umbrella? This scenario happened to me, by the way. To answer that thought in the back of your mind, no, I did not have an umbrella or enough gas.

Chances are, by this point in time in your life. You have completed a questionnaire or a set of behavioral questions that have asked you who you are and what you would do in a particular situation. You might not have noticed while you were getting frustrated at 100 questions about what you would do if Jimmy did XYZ because many of those questions were the same questions, just reworded.

Anticipate your answers to the questions that you know will be asked. Many of you, including myself, have interviewed for a job more than we've ever accepted them and not realizing that we should know the answers by now.

In the next chapter, I will list some interview questions for you to get to know. You will know what your answer should be and, most notably, how to say the right thing, the right way, and to get the best results.

Before we get started, with the hard work, remember that preparation is everything. Also, remember that if you fail to plan, you plan to fail. "Perfect Practice makes Perfect." This quote is from the best basketball player of all time, Micheal Jordan.

Lastly, this is for you to remember. I hope you're writing this down; by the way, there is no such thing as a one million dollar dream, but only a one million dollar execution.

All that said, it is not about how you start; instead, it's how you finish and follow through. So, to wrap up the 24-hour interview success system's expectations, it is to prepare, plan, practice, and perform.

(2)

Some questions that you want to ask yourself while you prepare are as followed,

Who am I?

What is important to me about a job?

How much money will I make?

Is money the end result for me being here?

Am I happy?

If I seek growth, is there room for growth for me here?

Is timing an issue for me with their work shifts?

Identifying who you are and what you are is critical during the preparation process. You need to ask yourself *do you want a job or do you want a career.* Write your goals down and make your goals straightforward and clear to read. If you have ever heard or made a vision board, this is your chance to use it.

When I was looking for a job, I had to know *what* I was looking for. Make a list of the responsibilities that you had in your past jobs. If you have had similar duties, then great. While you're making your list, you will begin to notice that you are starting to repeat certain **words over and over and over again.**

These words are called your **skills** from your job duties and are the answers to the next question. *What am I good at, and what am I great at?*

Something that I learned along the way of working with Fortune 500 companies may also have noticed it. In your job search, ten different companies are interested. Still, out of 10 companies, 5 of those results have the same job responsibilities. There is no coincidence here. Don't focus on the title when you are searching. Instead, focus your search on your commitment to the responsibilities.

What to learn from this is that the job title is not as important as the actual responsibilities. These different companies will call the same job other titles, but sometimes they're all the same.

Now, with that info, you can increase your open job opening searches by 20%. There may be different titles for the job market, but **the ingredients are the same.**

.

Making Sense? Career choices are improving now.

PLAN

How does your resume look? These repetitive words that you are writing down should also be placed aside later for your resume. Employers quickly want to know what you are good at and if it is valuable to them. Take your time and have your resume professionally typed for presentation.

Remember that your resume is your 15 seconds of fame. Think back to your favorite beverage's last commercial. The marketing department did not take 10 minutes to convince you that you are either thirsty or when you get thirsty that you will purchase their product.

A good resume writer can have your brand new resume completed in 2 to 3 business days and sometimes the same day. Resume writers can also take up to two weeks. Price ranges are from $20 to $1000. For an example of resume prices, visit Patterson Resume Resources at www.PattersonResumeResources.com

My team of HR professionals or myself will complete your resume and have you ready for your interview in no time. If you do your resume yourself, please be honest on your resume, make sure that it is polished and flows smoothly, and most importantly, proofread your work.

Secrets Revealed! Don't take the job description of your job and write it as the details of your job. It is ok to take specific phrases to make sure that you are in the right ballpark with the industry language.

It is not ok to give a recruiter the same description as the last ten people who applied for the same job. I want to know what **_YOU_** did and not what every *chemical analyst* or *cashier* did at the local employer.

I imagine you are trying to dictate what you do professionally and now have trouble elaborating on it. You go onto the internet and copy and paste a job description of the company website you used to work for and put it on your resume. Please don't do that!

On your resume, it is your opportunity to shine and brag on either how you make a difference or the substantial work you did. Remember, preparation before execution will save you a time that could have been a disaster.

How can creating positive business relationships while passively searching for employment be your secret weapon? This is easy!

When you meet new people, the first thing you don't want to do is ask what they can do for you but instead, what can you do for them. People love to talk about themselves and what they do. That is one of the best conversation pivot points into getting an **IN** with them.

This is called networking. A lot of people or organizations will not teach you how to network appropriately. Some *salesly* sounding friend or coworker of yours will tell you to go around to a bunch of strangers, shake their hands, and ask them to help you reach your goals.

But this is not the way to get people to remember you. You want people to go out of their way to help you because they want to. I have a system that would help you in this networking process, and its essence comes from President Kennedy. He simply said, "Ask not about what your country can do for you, but what you can do for your country." [7]

When we do things for people, don't think of them as favors, but you do want to think of everything you do as intentional from this point as an investment. *Do you have friends or associates that bring you value in your corner?* If you don't, then this is another opportunity to do an assessment of your assets.

If you have friends who are always asking you to do things for them and are not helping you when it is their turn, you know what to do.

Find communities related to your industry, the local college, or your college that you graduated from to see what resources are currently available for you. If you have a mentor or teacher from a previous internship that you invested a lot of your time and energy in, don't forget about them now.

This moment is your opportunity to reap every seed that you have sown professionally to reach your professional goals sooner than later. When I was looking for employment in Chicago a few years ago, I made a professional connection in a group on Facebook.

Without trying to have selfish intent or motive for the connection, this person went out of their way to send me job openings that matched my resume. Thank you, Ms. Wilson, for your support.

So think about the family that may already be working for the company you want to do for. Think about the friends that may know someone on the inside.

Also, consider your associates that work there or that used to work there because they may provide excellent insight for your next crucial steps. Leave no stone unturned.

(4)

DO THIS. (The System)

Use the chart included in this book to track contacts and movement. This chart is very similar to a systematic sales funnel chart to bring your leads down an extensive opening into an interview's most promising production.

When qualifying for job opportunities, ask yourself if your duties are still valuable. This year, jobs and processes have become more automated, and people are replaced by technology. Here is a theory, maybe expired skills are being replaced by tech, and your job expires because of it. It is essential to remain sharp and current on your skillset.

Using the Lead Funnel System is going to place valuable interviews in your schedule. Some may be over the phone, and some may communicate through email. But ultimately, the goal is to take it to the next level, which is the actual in-person meetup—the exchange of who is who and what is what.

You can do 65% of the work before you even leave your home. The key is to treat getting a job like it is your actual job. (With Breaks, no distractions, and with the expectations that you have a deadline to meet.) Eight hours a day of prep & execution will help you get to a start date much quicker.

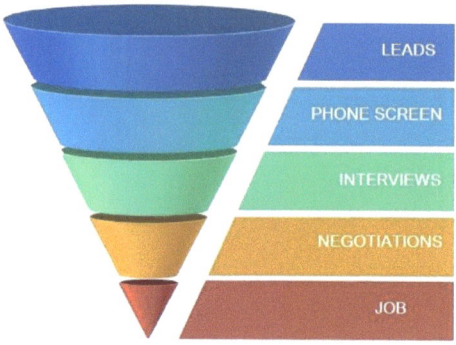

(3)

ASK YOURSELF.

Who are you, and whom do you want to be? **Knowing how to bridge those two gaps is strategically executing a career plan. To get from A to Z is where the fun comes in with a career coach or just sitting down and writing down your goals, dreams, and plans to execute.**

Do you need to refresh your skills with a contract job, or do you need to pick up another skill? **Only you can answer this.**

ASK YOURSELF.

Are you exhausting every resource possible? **College Career Center, Alumni, Industry communities, fraternities, sororities, associations, Career Development programs (non-profit & for-profit). Websites like LinkedIn,**

Glassdoor, Salary.com, CareerBuilder.com, Career Fairs, and Job Fairs.

Use all your resources to know what jobs or positions interest you in your city or commute range. All open opportunities aren't online or ready to apply. Some are in person or by invite/referral only.

Use the job market to your advantage. Know your local job market and who is in it. Inside the traditional job, markets are multiple generations. Each generation is a part of the cultural makeup of whom you work with, for, and for the purpose of this book, whom you will interview.

So how do you speak to them? How do you speak their language? What will be the best way for your application to get in front of his or her face?

It was hard for me to get employment, but I know that I needed to make the process easier. We all have our unique situations and reasons we need to find work. So with that being said, every excuse that you make places you two steps backward in your progress. Those two steps are getting through it and getting over yourself.

To be direct, I didn't always want to be an HR (Human Resources Consultant) or Staffing Specialist. When I graduated high school, I was just as lost and backward as a football stick at the volleyball race.

I went from customer service to culinary arts to military to psychology, marital counseling, back to cooking, to cooking and teaching again. My life was struck with disaster at home and landed me by sick father before he passed away.

So here I was with all of these random skills that didn't make sense together at first and back at home. In the city of Wilson, NC, the job market can be diverse. Still, if you don't have special training or higher education, you may have to be patient before finding gainful employment.

So I simplified my skill set and remembered what I was great at; Customer Service. Being the Jack or Jane of all trades will only make you as valuable as the other 10,000,000 people who want to be great and successful but don't know-how in your field.

You have to master something. Raises, promotions, and your career path begin when you begin to sharpen your skill set. The main thing is to start somewhere. You might be like me and have to go to the career buffet and try all the flavors before finding that special one.

(9)

I have a friend and teammate from one of the chambers of commerce leadership programs I completed. She is an excellent example of not being afraid of finding what you are great at. We call her "Karate Nurse," and if she hurts you in any way, be assured that she can heal you also.

Your professional identity will define your personal brand also. Knowing if what you are good at is your "professional hobby" or your passion will make a world of difference in how long you stay at that job.

Are your skills useful? There was a story that another career coach gave me about a football player that played quarterback.

To read off a few valuable bullet points: Passing yards 234, 115 touchdowns, 3,151 Rushing Yards, 40 Touch Downs, and this North Carolina quarterback has his degree. If this candidate wanted another job for any reason, he wouldn't make his $20 Million a year salary working at the local pizza place.

A person who is this type of valuable wouldn't work **eight months making dog food or building solar panels**. Although this candidate has an education, he is more than likely not the best candidate to perform open-heart surgery.

My point to it all is that when you are what you and your resume say, this is where you are more likely to succeed than you will have to relocate to where another quarterback is needed. That is the purpose of going where your skill is required and valued so that you don't spend 8-12 years waiting for your skillset to be useful again.

There was a shirt factory in my hometown and a HUGE layoff, followed by the factory shutting down. Unfortunately, shirt makers were out of a job. These workers' only options had been to move to another area where shirts are made or pick up another trade or skill useful in this area.

For years, unemployment was drawn because some waited for their skills to be useful again, but that didn't happen. Know your value, worth, and identity. Go where you are relevant, or get a new skill. Unless you are great at economic analysis or predicting the stock market, don't plan to wait around for the opportunity. **Go Get It!**

This moment is your chance to bring out your favorite crayons and pencils and pens and just getting messy on a clean slate. So the hard work is done, well, kinda.

Planning is the portion of the process that goes rather quickly, but it is equally important.

Ask yourself do you want to work in state or out of state. Also, ask yourself, do you qualify for the job that you currently wish to have. As a recruiter, I have seen people apply for jobs that they were only good at in their minds. And if I haven't said it just yet, we as recruiters can be very short-sighted, **QUICK TO JUDGE. It only takes seven seconds** to keep a resume in front of us or place it in the **"Not Today Pile"** {Use your imagination where this pile is.} It doesn't matter if the resume is 1-2 pages. It should only take **one minute** to read from top to bottom.

If you haven't thought about it, you are one of many when you apply for a job. If you apply at a temp agency, you are more than likely the **101ˢᵗ** person to inquire about the job. So, roughly a pound of resumes come in. We have to filter out the best of the best to consider interviewing or prescreening.

Out of the **101** people to apply or submit their resume to a job, **20** applicants have the skills and experience necessary for the job. Out of the **20** that have the skills, **10** applicants have an accurate history, skills, and accurate contact information for us to call.

Out of the **10** candidates with those juicy pieces of info, **6** candidates have the current telephone number and email address updated. Out of the **6** candidates left in this process, **4** are available for an interview and may get the **1ˢᵗ** round of interviews set.

So out of the **4** left from **101** applicants, **1** of you lied on your resume, and **1** may have less than favorable background check results. So the **2** best applicants will become candidates for the position and compete against each other for a second interview. The process starts entirely over the next day, and **100** fresh applicants go through the same process. Happy Hunger Games, and may the odds be ever in your favor.

There is a process to find the right person, and I am not sharing this to scare you. Before you speak to a headhunter, sourcing specialist, recruiter, or human resources representative, I want you to know that it was a journey just to get to that first call to you.

I promise that I am NOT trying to complicate things or make it harder for you. The HR representative had five candidates on reserve before posting the position and another **ten** candidates that worked there currently and applied. (And a set of internally referred applicants)

Understand that before you send an email or pick up the phone to express interest, you need to plan your attack and approach better than the other 100 that want the job that you want. So what is the secret to interviewing more and applying less? Planning, of course! Merely doing this step will make your results more potent.

Know what you're applying for after getting to know who you are. Sometimes the job descriptions or titles can be confusing. Account Managers, for example, over 40 types of Account Managers combined with most industries.

The best way to be effective in the planning phase is to use the results you finished with during the identification process.

Resume SEO

Have you ever heard of **Resume SEO**? RSEO is not a common term. Very few people have spoken these words together. **Resume Search Engine Optimization** is the **Super Tool** to drive employers to find you.

Now, what is resume search engine optimization?

Search engine optimization is the process of optimizing or increasing the visibility of content through search engines. How Resume SEO helps you is easy. Think about the last time you looked something up on Google. You put in a keyword, and everything about that thing popped up, right? And more than likely, you click on the one out of a millionth item that has the best headline.

So think of that same method with your resume. Make sure that your resume has useful and relevant keywords and terms throughout your resume. Make sure you have an eye-catching headline that would make you stand out compared to the rest. Suppose you can use relevant hyperlinks, like LinkedIn or an online portfolio or even a video cover letter, available at vloggedin.com. In that case, you may include on-demand personal videos by listing those links on your profiles and resumes.

Ensure that your social media profiles are clean. The content you want recruiters to find on your profiles should be relevant or improves the perception of how they view you. If you want to post what you want regardless of employers searching for you, you could change your name, so the recruiter doesn't find you easily. On Instagram, the kids call this a Finsta. Finsta is a combined word meaning fake Instagram. Fake + Instagram = FInsta

Here is a **Challenge**. Search for **Travis C. Patterson** or **CoachTCP** on Twitter, Facebook, LinkedIn, Google, Yahoo, or any search engine. My personal and professional brand should be consistent and perpetual. My brand is hire-ready. Let us be hire-ready.

Something **new** that many people are not doing yet to be competitive is making a **Video Cover Letter**. There are sites like vloggedin.com that will allow you to record yourself and make the video so that only the person who has the link can view it. You can also do this with youtube.com as well. Just set the link to unlisted when you publish it.

Record a video introducing yourself to an employer or specific company representative and place it on your resume as a hyperlink. The link should direct to your video with the words on the document reading **Cover Letter Link** or **Cover Letter** or **Cover Letter Video**. This method is a surefire way to stand out, be original, and say all the RIGHT things that you feel that you couldn't say on paper.

Not comfortable with how to do it or say the right words, call me for coaching. We can set up a video call.

Google Search CoachTCP Elevator Pitch or CoachTCP Video Cover Letter, and you will see an example. It is SUPER EASY. I promise.

Practice

Perfect practice makes perfect. I first heard that phrase from the best basketball player of all time. I also listened to another quote from a famous ear-biting boxer, and the quote went, "Everyone has a plan until they get in the ring and get punched in the face." Taking that quote is that you MUST also have to prepare for failure when you prepare for success.

Communication is essential throughout this process. In the first interview, you are setting the tone for the next interview and how he or she will remember you. Please don't be forgettable, but don't be recognized for doing too much during your interview. Set the scene and the tone. This is why practicing at home, with a friend or a trusted professional, is essential.

When you plan your offense, you also have to plan for defense. One of the biggest mistakes that I have made going into an interview is being too confident. People say that doctors are the worst patients. I think that same thing goes for people who interview are the worst interviewees. I walked in thinking because I knew all the answers they were looking for that the job would magically fall in my lap. I didn't plan for their observation on how I responded versus what I said. When I was younger, my answer to every can you question, was *of course,* or *yes, I can* regardless of whether I could complete the task.

This company used software daily, and I verbally said that I could use this program. I was not expecting them to have a demo of the program in the next room to assess my knowledge. I failed.

So on that note, I want to start this section off by saying *tell the truth*. I'm not saying be boring, but make sure you are truthful. Below you will see examples of questions that you are more than likely to ask in your interview. They are called behavioral interview questions.

The goal is to learn what your behavior was during specific scenarios. In behavioral interview questions, the goal is to use the preparation and planning you have done before using truthful answers. If you know yourself and you know your value, you will never have to oversell yourself to anyone.

Practice in the mirror and on camera if you can, or even in front of a friend how to answer these types of questions.

The remedy for all of these questions is called STAR.

STAR a technique that stands for situation task action and results. You're going to want to explain the situation after hearing the question and then re-quote what the actual task or problem was given to you to solve. Tactfully and directly explain your action to how you solve that problem and finished off by presenting the results of the action you provided to the tax given to you and the situation you previously explained.

(3)

This is an example of STAR. This scenario is from a client I had this year. He is a Service Manager at his local dealership.

(3)

Tell me about a
time when you took
the lead on a
difficult project?"

A few years back I was working as a
Service Advisor at car dealership. One
morning in our department staff meeting
the Service Manager announced that we had
been receiving an unacceptable amount of
negative reviews for the service we had
been providing our customers. His solution
was to create a committee that would
analyze the situation and put forth
actionable improvements, and for this he
asked for volunteers.

I had been looking for an opportunity to
show that I was capable of taking on more
responsibility, and being a person who
enjoys working in group situations, I was
the first to volunteer. My Service Manager
was quick to make me the leader of the
committee, which put me in the position of
the leader of a group of 4 other people who
were tasked to come up with a solution.

S.T.A.R.
Situation

S.T.A.R
Task

(3)

Over the next three weeks we analyzed each of the customer services reports and discovered that the vast majority of negative reviews were a result of lengthy wait times for customers. Knowing that we had to come up with a solution to decrease the amount of time our customers were left waiting, I then lead brainstorming sessions to find a way to fix the problem. We zoned in on changing the way our mechanics worked on each work order.

S.T.**A**.R Action

After implementing my suggestion, mechanics were able to focus mainly on their specializations, which meant they worked faster and more efficiently, which translated to wait times dropping by 18%. This was a situation that required me to manage 4 people and find a solution that created a positive outcome and solved a critical issue, which I believe I was able to do.

S.T.A.**R**. Results

(4)

If you missed any of our Interview Workshops, here are some questions from the workbook. Practice using the STAR technique below.

Tell me a little about yourself. Because this is often the opening question, be careful that you don't run off at the mouth. Keep your answer to a minute or two, and consider four topics:
- ❖ Early Years
- ❖ Education
- ❖ Work History
- ❖ Recent Career Experience

_____
_____
_____
_____
_____
_____
_____
_____
_____

Why should we hire you?

❖ Create your answer by thinking in terms of your ability, your experience, and your energy.

_____

_____

_____

_____

_____

_____

_____

_____

_____

_____

_____

_____

_____

_____

_____

_____

_____

_____

_____

_____

_____

_____

_____

_____

_____

_____

_____

_____

If you could start your career over again, what would you do differently? The best answer is, "Not a thing."

- ❖ You should try to present yourself as a person who is happy with his or her life.

- ❖ You've enjoyed its ups and learned from its downs.

- ❖ As a result, you would not want to change things that brought you to where you are today.

- ❖ Mention that it is the past after all, that has prepared you for this position.

_____

_____

_____

_____

_____

_____

_____

_____

_____

_____

_____

_____

_____

_____

_____

_____

_____

_____

_____

_____

What career options do you have at this moment?

- ❖ You should try to identify three areas of interest, one of which includes this company and job.

- ❖ The other two should be in related fields.

_____

_____

_____

_____

_____

_____

_____

_____

_____

_____

_____

_____

_____

_____

_____

_____

_____

_____

_____

_____

_____

_____

_____

_____

If you could choose any company, where would you go?

❖ Talk about the job and the company for which you are being interviewed.

_____

_____

_____

_____

_____

_____

_____

_____

_____

_____

_____

_____

_____

_____

_____

_____

_____

_____

_____

_____

_____

_____

_____

_____

_____

How long will you stay with us?

❖ Say that you are interested in a career with the organization, but admit that you would have to continue to feel challenged to remain with an organization. Think in terms of, "As long as we both feel achievement-oriented."

In your current (last) position, what features do (did) you like the most? The least?

Be careful and be positive. Describe more features that you liked than disliked.

- ❖ Don't cite personality problems.
- ❖ Suppose you make your last job sound terrible. In that case, an interviewer could wonder why you did you remain there until now or whether you are the bad apple that would raise issues in the new company.

_____

_____

_____

_____

_____

_____

_____

_____

_____

_____

_____

_____

_____

_____

_____

_____

_____

_____

_____

_____

_____

_____

Why are you leaving (did leave) your present (last) position?
Be brief, to the point, and as honest as you can without
hurting yourself.

- ❖ Refer back to your job search's planning phase, where
  you considered this topic as you thought about
  reference statements.
- ❖ Otherwise, indicate that the move was your decision,
  the result of your desire to advance your career.
- ❖ Don't mention personality conflicts.
- ❖ The interviewer may spend some time probing you on
  this issue, mainly if it's clear that you were
  terminated. Be as positive and honest as you can. The
  "We agreed to disagree" approach may be useful.
- ❖ Don't fabricate a story for an interview; even in
  today's climate, your story may be checked.

_____

_____

_____

_____

_____

_____

_____

_____

_____

_____

_____

_____

_____

_____

_____

_____

_____

Why haven't you found a job before now?

Say that finding a job isn't difficult, but that finding the right job deserves time and demands careful planning.

_____

_____

_____

_____

_____

_____

_____

_____

_____

_____

_____

_____

_____

_____

_____

_____

For more examples of questions and responses, follow this link to more info at www.traviscpatterson.com

Perform

"Work The Plan, Or Plan To Work." - Wes Brown, Financial Advisor & Expert

"Expect the unexpected. Don't let emotions get in the way of decision making."- Ryan Simons, Wilson Chamber of Commerce President, Wilson, NC

"Building a visionary company requires one percent vision and 99 percent alignment." - Jim Collins and Jerry Porras, Built to Last

"Without a strategy, execution is aimless. Without execution, the strategy is useless." - Morris Change, CEO of TSMC

"Strategy is a pattern in a stream of decisions" - Henry Mintzberg

"The Journey is more important than the destination" - Ryan Gladieux, President of a Plastics Company in Wilson, NC

Now you have prepared for this moment, and here we are, time to use what you planned and practice and execute the performance.

Many inspirational speakers, company presidents, and CEOs have told me this one consistent piece of advice. When reaching your goals to become the best you can be, remember that the process is more important than the product. The process is more important than the product. **The journey is more important than the destination.**

We need to be the hungry type to be successful when it comes to reaching our career goals. Some people know their journey and are energized by it to obtain every promotion and career level they go after. Own your story. Own your history. Own your skills and strength, and most importantly, know your value.

When you know the process of being you and how you became the best you can be, there is no longer a need to fake who you are in the interview. Becoming genuine is excellent and an honor.

The rules are simple **to get an interview in 24 hours or less**; you have to treat **getting a job like an actual job**. *Let me say that again, and you have to treat getting a job like it is your job.*

What do I mean? 8 to 12 hours, you need to build your interview funnel by sourcing your communities, your friends, your family, online communities, websites, colleges, your alumni, and career coaches like myself. If you have the opportunity to have a mentor or internship, use them for information and leads.

What is the interview funnel? The figure below *(3)* is a picture of a funnel with a wide top that drops leads and opportunities down a vast whole and at the bottom is filtered by the best and most intentional results.

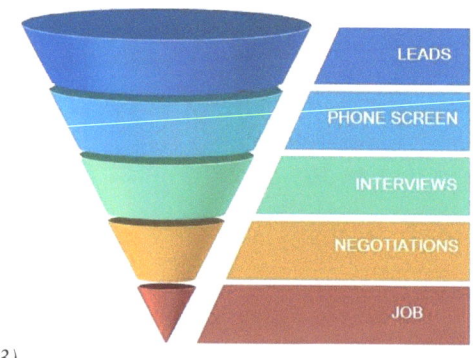

(3)

Now while you are working your 8 to 12-hour shift, getting job interviews, and accepting job interviews because of your new SEO Resume, write everything that happens during your interview process down. Below is a copy of a form format that you can use to keep track of every person you connect with and contact.

Be prepared to speak to more gatekeepers than decision-makers. Gatekeepers are the people who answer the phone or meet you at the front desk to direct you to the next step of the hiring process or to tell you that they are not hiring. So when you receive nine **NO**'s, prepare for that one **YES**! Sometimes you have to take **NO** and hear that **NO** as they are not hiring you right **now**.

This is no disrespect to anyone who is the secretary, receptionist, or assistant. Please believe that I have had all three roles in my time. Gatekeepers filter the calls and walk through traffic so the decision-maker can save more time and do more work. *I have been the gatekeeper, the recruiter, the hiring manager, and it all started with a job interview.*

This secret is the biggest secret that I can give you when it comes to getting past gatekeepers, and it is merely this. *Go to* www.linkedin.com *and create an account and type in the company's name and the city that they reside in to find the decision maker's name.* **Practice** saying this person's name and how you ask for him or her before you call to sound like you already know them, and they are **expecting you**.

This step is where the **practicing** has come in handy. Be strong, confident, and genuine and who you are.

Please don't arrive in the parking lot **15** minutes before the interview. Please arrive **20** to **30** minutes early in the waiting area waiting on your upcoming interview. The same strategy works for phone interviews. Make sure you are in a quiet place and not driving. Also, don't hang around distractions before the call.

Make sure your head is in the game, and wait for them to call you. Be in a situation when you are prepared ahead of time for this call if he or she gets you early. Remember the interview question, ***what are your current options***. Don't sound like you are showboating as if you have another interview in 1 hour, so you rush the interviewer.

In every interview, give your **100%** attention and respect to the interview. It is respectful to tell your interviewer (when asked) that you are interviewing for the same position at another company. The pay is better, or the benefits are better if it is true. To be **competitive,** remember this statement when they ask you about your upcoming schedule or job interviews with other companies. You can say you have waited for this current opportunity to interview with them and the company. If they have a start date, in negotiation, tell them you will decline your current job offers for and offer letter with this company."

Preparation could be necessary here to prepare questions for your interviewer and read about the companies activities or even meet the interview earlier if they reach out to you. Be unforgettable but not in a wrong way. Be remembered for dressing for success, saying all the right things, and being enthusiastic about the opportunity to join the company.

A mistake that I made once for a job interview was unwise and immature. The interview was 3 hours away in Charlotte, North Carolina, and I did not prepare for the rain, the traffic. I was so embarrassed when during the interview. I feel like I said all the right things, but I was covered in the rain and out of breath because I was almost late.

It's easy to make this mistake no matter what age you are but don't be too honest. Don't tell the interviewer that you were late because you have diarrhea. Don't say to the interviewer that you are without employment for consuming unpaid inventory because you were eating the donuts in the bakery listed on your resume.

When the interviewer asks you why we should hire you, please don't say because I have nine children and need the money. Imagine some of you right now saying that could be the truth, but if money drives you, you can find it anywhere.

Do a huge favor for me? Leave your phone in the car or leave it at home until you get back if it is too hot. STAY FOCUSED and Leave Your Excuses at the DOOR! You can only give 100% to one activity at a time.

(3) (4)

CoachTCP.com will take you to TravisCPatterson.com

You'll find book resources at TheInterviewAccelerator.com

Here is a **BONUS**!

If you also want to Learn …

How To Negotiate Your Salary...

How Can Failures Make You More Successful…

Go to www.TheInterviewAccelerator.com

Please let me know what you think! I will personally read your reviews and thoughts if you send them directly to me. Send them to

info@TheInterviewAccelerator.com

Attached are the Interview Lead Sheets [5],

Download additional lead sheets and more resources at

www.TheInterviewAccelerator.com

CoachTCP's Interview Lead System

Date	Company Name	Time	Telephone Number	How Did You Hear About The Position?	Listed Contact Person	Gate Keeper	Decision Maker (If Different From	Any one Refer You?	Results of Call or Email
00/00/2016	Wilson Resume Writers	11:25AM	508-266-5365	CoachTCP.com	Nicole	Shae	Travis C. Patterson	Sarah-Grace	1st Interview 00/00/2016, 01:00hm with Nicole
Total									

(5),

CoachTCP's Interview Lead System

Date	Company Name	Time	Telephone Number	How Did You Hear About The Position?	Listed Contact Person	Gate Keeper	Decision Maker (if Different From	Any one Refer You?	Results of Call or Email
00/00/2016	Wilson Resume Writers	1:25AM	508-266-5365	CoachTCP.com	Nicole	Shae	Travis C. Patterson	Sarah-Grace	1st Interview 00/00/2016, 01:00am with Nicole
Total									

(5),

(5),

CoachTCP's Interview Lead System

Date	Company Name	Time	Telephone Number	How Did You Hear About The Position?	Listed Contact Person	Gate Keeper	Decision Maker (If Different From	Any one Refer You?	Results of Call or Email
00/00/2016	Wilson Resume Writers	11:25AM	508-266-5365	CoachTCP.com	Nicole	Shae	Travis C. Patterson	Sarah Grace	1st Interview 00/00/2016, 01:00pm with Nicole
Total									

(5),

CoachTCP's Interview Lead System

Date	Company Name	Time	Telephone Number	How Did You Hear About The Position?	Listed Contact Person	Gate Keeper	Decision Maker (if Different From	Any one Refer You?	Results of Call or Email
00/00/2016	Wilson Resume Writers	11:25AM	508-266-5365	CoachTCP.com	Nicole	Shae	Travis C. Patterson	Sarah-Grace	1st Interview 00/00/2016, 01:00pm with Nicole
Total									

(5),

CoachTCP's Interview Lead System

Date	Company Name	Time	Telephone Number	How Did You Hear About The Position?	Listed Contact Person	Gate Keeper	Decision Maker (if Different From	Any one Refer You?	Results of Call or Email
00/00/2016	Wilson Resume Writers	11:25AM	508-266-5365	CoachTCP.com	Nicole	Shae	Travis C. Patterson	Sarah-Grace	1st Interview 00/00/2016, 01:00bm with Nicole

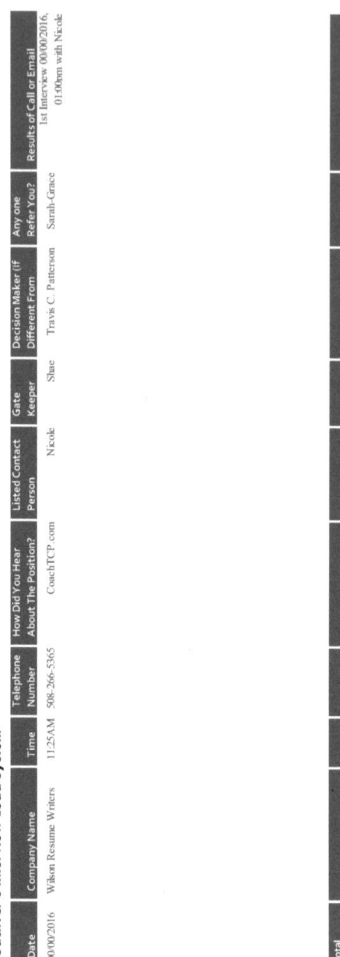

Total

The Author

Travis C. Patterson is an Author, Speaker, and Interview Coach with founded company PRR Training & Consulting, formally doing business as Wilson Resume Writers.

Featured In Yahoo, Influncive, and other international publications, Travis also goes by CoachTCP and has over ten years of industry-related training & experience in Interview Coaching, Resume Writing, Recruitment, Staffing, Workforce Development, Talent Acquisition, Confidence Coaching, and Communication Improvement.

Travis has spoken on personal and professional development to government, private and public for-profit and not-for-profit organizations. Travis is a 20 Under 40 & NAACP award winner. He is considered a top subject expert and authority on Interview Execution & Interview Preparation.

(3) (4)

Resources:

www.TravisCPatterson.com

www.TheInterviewAccelerator.com

www.CoachTCP.com >>> (Traviscpatterson.com)

Free Podcast:

The Interview Accelerator: Guarantee Your Next Interview

The podcast is published on Pandora, Google Podcast, Apple Podcasts, and other podcast publishing platforms.

To access your free trial to The Interview Accelerator interview coaching platform, visit:

www.theinterviewaccelerator.com/7-day-trial-the-interview-accelerator/

www.ingramcontent.com/pod-product-compliance
Lightning Source LLC
Chambersburg PA
CBHW040836180526
45159CB00001B/213